Trading Panic for Peace
a study of the 23rd Psalm

Kristen Sauder

D1279578

PRESS

Dedication

. . . .

I am so grateful for my Shepherd Whose goodness overflows in my life in the form of the World's Best Husband and four absolutely precious kids, Olivia, Drew, Ivy and Ellie, who give me tons of support and plenty of good illustrations!

I am also filled with gratitude for the sisters in Christ who encouraged me to compile these lessons in book form. So it is to a special group of ladies who piloted this study last summer and to my life-long friend, Valerie, who hosted the crowd in her home that I dedicate this finished product!

Trading Panic for Peace

· · · · · · · · · · · · · · · ·

Contents

"Brown paper packages tied up with string. These are a few of my favorite things." I'll bet you're humming along! Most of us are familiar with this tune made famous by the movie "The Sound of Music." And, I'd have to agree, packages are some of my favorite things, when they're addressed to me!

My mom is one of the best package packers there's ever been. She can cram more tiny treasures and delightful goodies in one small parcel than imaginable. She possesses a knack for finding just the right thing, always personal and full of meaning. When the mailman delivers a box from Grammie the entire Sauder household, kids and adults alike, hover in anticipation.

Who doesn't like getting a box in the mail? Remember receiving care packages in college? At my university, students were given a slip in their PO Box telling them to pick up a package at the counter. If you got the slip it was your lucky day.

However, packages sent to the unknown girl with the PO Box next to yours weren't terribly exciting. As a matter of fact they were almost depressing. You could fantasize about the contents and even begin to drool as the smell of homemade chocolate chip cookies wafted your way, but you couldn't have any. It wasn't for you.

Ladies, God's Word is His gift to you. Every time you unzip your Bible cover and dig into the contents you'll be delighted to uncover treasures of every kind. One friend calls them gold nuggets. Yes, God's Book is full of them. As you turn the pages you'll discover you're encouraged, challenged, strengthened, changed, refreshed and renewed.

Every goody contained within God's Word has been specifically selected with you in mind. Each word of every verse is packed with power and chosen by the Author for maximum impact. After all, *"God's word is quick and powerful, sharper than any two edged sword,"* Hebrews 4:12. NASB

As you dive into Psalm 23 it's my prayer that you will enjoy unwrapping all that God Himself has packaged for you, and in so doing you will begin the trade — Panic for Peace!

Chapter One

Peace is a Person

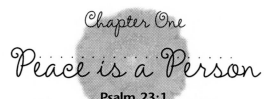

We're going to start at the very beginning and literally unwrap these treasures one word at a time.

The Lord is my shepherd, I shall not want. NASB

David opens this Psalm with a little word, very common, and easily overlooked, the word *the*. Yet, we began this study with the idea that every word of God is a gift chosen specifically by Him for your good. So, what can you learn from the article *the*? What difference does it make in the meaning of this verse? What does it imply?

_____

_____

_____

> *The world could get along without many a large book better than this sunny little Psalm.*
>
> *~Alexander McClaren*

I've asked this question many times in teaching Psalm 23 and most often the answer comes back that there is one Lord. Maybe your response pointed to this truth as well.

By using *the* David describes one Lord. He didn't say, "*A lord is my shepherd*" or "*One of the lords* is my shepherd." This becomes even more evident when we realize that the word for Lord in this first verse of Psalm 23 is the Hebrew word Yehovah. Strongs' Concordance defines Yehovah as, "the self Existent or Eternal, Jehovah, Jewish national name of God, Jehovah, the Lord."

Hold your place in Psalm 23 and turn back to Exodus chapter 20.

God says of Himself in Exodus 20:2-3

I am the Lord your God. ...You shall have no other gods before Me.

From the very beginning of Psalm 23 David lets us know with Whom we're dealing—the One true God. In David's day belief in one God was not popular. Outside of Israel idol worship was rampant and many nations worshiped multiple gods. Doesn't sound much different from our world today, does it?

David's bold statement, *The Lord is my shepherd,* set him apart. How has your faith in one Lord affected your daily life and your relationships with family members, co-workers and friends who don't share the same belief?

_____

_____

_____

_____

As we dwell in a world that is increasingly hostile to the truth of One God, we sometimes begin to panic. Have you ever found yourself asking questions like:

- *"What if I don't have all the right answers to defend my faith?"*

- *"How will I handle opposition without loosing my temper?"*

- *"Why is it that every time I take a stand for something I believe I'm offending someone?"*

✽ *"What kind of persecution will I face, or will my children face, in the days ahead?"*

What other fears begin to play out in your mind when you look at the world around you?

_____

_____

_____

_____

Corrie Ten Boon, a holocaust survivor, said, *"If you look at the world you'll be distressed. If you look within you'll be depressed. But if you look at Christ you'll be at rest."*

We may not be politically correct by holding to the truth of one God, but we can be incredibly confident.

In our home we have a verse we repeat often when faced with trying or terrifying circumstances. *"God is for me. I will not fear. What can man do to me?"* The words stick best with motions. It goes like this:

> *"If you look at the world you'll be distressed. If you look within you'll be depressed. But if you look at Christ you'll be at rest."*
> ~Corrie Ten Boon, Holocaust Survivor

God *(point to the heavens)*
is for *(hold up four fingers)*
me. *(point to yourself)*
I *(touch your eye)*
will not fear. *(shake your head no)*
What can man do to *(hold up two fingers)*
me? *(point to yourself)*   ~Psalm 118:6 NASB

Did you try it? I hope you'll practice this until you have it down pat, because peace will stamp out your panic when you remember that God is for you. He is your shepherd. You have no reason to fear.

David found this to be reality in his life. In essence David is doing a little bragging in Psalm 23:1. He's name dropping with a mighty impressive name!

During a special conference in Bible College, my husband Kurt was asked to shuttle speakers and musicians between their hotels and campus. I was excited to ride along and meet some of these well known Christian leaders. Although most of them would not begin to remember us, it's been tempting at different times in ministry to say, "Oh, so-and-so. I've met him." There's an element of prestige in being even remotely connected to fame.

In Psalm 23:1, it's as if David is relishing in his tie to the Famous One saying, "I don't know who your shepherd is, but THE Lord is my shepherd." The Almighty, the Creator of Heaven and earth, the all-powerful, all-knowing, eternal God is my shepherd. Wow!

When are you most pleased to be associated with your Shepherd?

_____

_____

_____

_____

Ladies, if you have placed your faith in Jesus Christ, if you are trusting Him alone as Savior, then you can confidently proclaim with David, *the Lord is my shepherd,* and if God is for us, who can be against us (Romans 8:31)?

The Lord is my shepherd...

Notice that David says, *the Lord is my shepherd.* Not maybe. Not He might be, but he *is my shepherd.* You have His personal promise in Hebrews 13:5. Turn there now and copy your promise on the lines that follow.

_____

_____

_____

_____

No matter what happens in your lifetime or in generations to follow, you have this hope: the Lord is your shepherd and He will never leave you nor forsake you. He is your Peace!

Isn't this exciting? We haven't even arrived at the end of the first sentence of Psalm 23 and already we've unwrapped so much. There's tons more, so glance again at Psalm 23:1.

The Lord is my shepherd...

Not only is David confident that the Lord is his shepherd, but he asserts, *the Lord is my shepherd.* Thank goodness, this is getting personal!

> The sweetest words of the whole is that monosyllable 'my'. He does not say, the Lord is the Shepherd of the world at large, and leadeth forth the multitude as His flock. He is a shepherd to me.
> ~Charles Spurgeon

Charles Spurgeon comments, *"The sweetest words of the whole is that monosyllable 'my'. He does not say, the Lord is the Shepherd of the world at large, and leadeth forth the multitude as His flock. He is a shepherd to me."*

The Lord is your personal shepherd.

Sometimes our panic isn't prompted by the world around us. Often it oozes out from within our own hearts like puss from a stubborn wound.

There's an old hymn I sung growing up, "Just as I Am." Maybe you're familiar with it. One stanza talks about "fightings and fears within, without." World events can be unsettling, but it's my daily self struggles that regularly give me fits. Have you ever wrestled with any of these peace nabbers?

- ❀ Feeling that God is distant
- ❀ Struggling to believe God could really love you
- ❀ Feeling condemned by God for all your sins and inadequacies
- ❀ Controlled by the need to earn God's favor
- ❀ Discouraged because you can't seem to connect with Him as deeply as you desire

God is so, well, God, that it's often hard to fathom that He desires a personal, daily relationship with us. Yet, everything He's said and all that He's done from the beginning of time demonstrates His longing for intimacy.

He is not just the Creator of the Universe. Not only the Savior of the world. He is your shepherd. Say it out loud right now just as David said it when he penned the Psalm:

❧ *The Lord is _my_ shepherd.*

What is keeping you from getting to know your Shepherd on a more personal level?

_____

_____

_____

We absolutely cannot continue without highlighting the word "shepherd" and his connection to the sheep. What comes to mind when you think of a shepherd?

_____

_____

_____

The image of a shepherd conjures up lively pictures in my mind. With little effort, I'm standing beside him in the field, drawing in deep lung-fulls of the great outdoors. Sunshine warms me almost to a sweat. My ears are teased by the many offerings—birds singing, the breeze rustling tree leaves, bees buzzing and, of course, the sound of sheep all around.

Perhaps you chose to describe a shepherd by his job description, and we will talk more about that. But, one thing is for certain, we can't muse for long about shepherds without thinking of sheep.

Interesting, isn't it, that not once in Psalm 23 does David say, "I am a sheep." It doesn't roll of the tongue too easily. _The Lord is my shepherd_ certainly sounds much better.

Yet, if the Lord is my shepherd, the obvious implication is that I am a sheep. And all of God's people said, "Baa." As humbling as our role may be in this little drama David has established, God is the Shepherd and we are His sheep.

Study these references in Scripture that refer to us as sheep.
Jot down your observations.

Jeremiah 50:6 _____

_____

_____

Matthew 10:16 _____

_____

_____

Matthew 26:31 _____

_____

_____

John 10:1-16 _____

_____

_____

What are some similarities between a child of God and a
sheep?

_____

_____

_____

Phillip Keller, former shepherd and author of *A Shepherd Looks at Psalm 23* says, *"Sheep do not 'just take care of themselves' as some might suppose. They require more than any other class of livestock, endless attention and meticulous care. It is no accident that God has chosen to call us sheep. Our mass mind (or mob instincts), our fears and timidity, our stubbornness and stupidity, our perverse habits are all parallels of profound importance."*

We'll have a greater opportunity to delve into our sheepish selves as we continue in Psalm 23, but for now, suffice it say that sheep we are.

And, sheep need a shepherd. As a matter of fact, sheep without a shepherd are a panicked lot in deed! *One of the best ways to trade our panic for peace is to realize all that we have in our Good Shepherd.*

Read Psalm 23:1 again,

The Lord is my shepherd, I shall not want. NASB

Accurately translated, *I shall not want* can be read, I shall not be in want. In other words, I shall not be in a state of want.

In recent years I've adopted a practice of not reading the newspaper sale flyers on Sunday. Advertisements ruin any sense of God focus my Sunday may otherwise have. One perusal through the pages of bargains at the local discount store and I find myself in a state of want! All at once I have so many "needs" I never knew I had.

How can discontentment rob us of our peace and invite panic to take up residency in our lives?

_____

_____

_____

David directly connects his ability to be content, or to not be in want, to the fact that the Lord is his shepherd. How can knowing that the Lord is your shepherd help you experience peace through contentment?

A sheep with a poor shepherd has reason for concern, but a sheep with a Good Shepherd is content.

The Lord is qualified to be your shepherd.

1. He made you.
2. He paid for you (with the blood of Christ Jesus His Son).
3. He cares for you daily.

Someone once said, "When we get to the end of all we have we find He is all we need."

Your need is the beginning point of a satisfying relationship with your Shepherd. Why not admit afresh your need for a shepherd. Use this space to record a personal prayer of surrender to and gratitude for your Good Shepherd.

Go Deep, Sheep!

Spiritual Discipline to Practice: Simplicity

Scripture Passage: 1 Timothy 6:6-10

Maintenance of stuff siphons valuable time and precious energy.

- ❀ Ask, "Is this a want or a need?" before each purchase.

- ❀ If you add one thing, subtract another.

- ❀ Regularly give away things you don't use to others in need.

- ❀ Fast occasionally from shopping or spending on extras. See how long you can go before you absolutely buy out of necessity!

Verse to Memorize: 1 Timothy 6:6
"But godliness with contentment is great gain."

Notes

Notes

Notes

Chapter Two
A Peace-filled Pace
Psalm 23:2

He __makes__ me lie down...

Why is it that parents enjoy naps but children don't? Now that I'm all grown up a little mid day shut-eye is a rare treat, but as a child I dreaded Dad's after lunch instructions to lie down and rest when we were on family vacation. In spite of all the whining by my three siblings and me Dad would insist. Our pleading sounded something like this:

Kids: *Why do we have to?*
Dad: *You don't have to. You get to.*
Kids: *How long do we have to?*
Dad: *Until you fall asleep.*
Kids: *But, we can't fall asleep.*
Dad: *You'll just have to try.*
Kids: *We're not tired...zzz!*

About an hour and a half or so later we'd all be awake again!

> O God! Thou hast made us for Thyself and our souls are restless, searching, 'til they find their rest in Thee.
>
> ~Saint Augustine of Africa

*He **makes** me lie down.* That's not an invitation, and it doesn't give the impression of a suggestion. Why do you think David uses the word "makes" here?

_____

_____

_____

Like a child who keeps going until he falls over from exhaustion rather than stopping for rest, we often charge stubbornly through life without prioritizing the renewal we require.

Like a child who keeps going until he falls over from exhaustion rather than stopping for rest, we often charge stubbornly through life without prioritizing the renewal we require.

Jesus whispers, *Come to Me, all who are weary and heavy-laden, and I will give you rest...you shall find rest for your souls.* (Matthew 11:28-29 NASB)

Rest for our souls, doesn't that sound wonderful? When will we step off the treadmill and take Jesus up on His offer?

The country music group Alabama describes life's crazy pace: *"I'm in a hurry to get things done. Oh, I rush and rush until life's no fun. All I really gotta do is live and die. But I'm in a hurry and don't know why."*

On one particular trip to Grandma and Grandpa's farm we received news that necessitated an earlier return home than expected. All of our kids were sorely disappointed to miss the fun times planned with friends and family. Our daughter, Ivy, came up with a plan. "We could just ram it all into today," she suggested.

You know, that's how many of us live our lives, ramming everything possible into today. Of course all that we want to do and plan to do never fits into one day, so we string together a series of impossibly busy days, months and years.

Many times our Good Shepherd will allow the circumstances of our lives to facilitate a much-needed season of rest. Has God ever used one or more of the following to slow you down?

- ❀ The loss of a job
- ❀ A move
- ❀ An illness
- ❀ A family crisis
- ❀ Other: _____

Do you ever argue with God about needing rest? When God makes you "lie down", what are some of the excuses you use to assure Him you don't need a break?

_____

_____

_____

Can you give an example of a time when the Lord caused you to stop and rest and it turned out to be the very thing you needed?

_____

_____

_____

How can you take advantage of the soul rest the Lord offers on a more regular basis?

_____

_____

_____

He not only *makes me lie down,* but He makes me lie down *in green pastures...*

In terms of a shepherd and his sheep the phrase "makes me lie down" also carries the understanding that the shepherd is making it possible for his sheep to lie down. Sheep are easily panicked and find rest difficult to come by unless they have a reason for peace.

The setting has to be right. The pastures have to be green. Green pastures along with the presence of the shepherd pave the way for peace.

Phillip Keller points out in *A Shepherd Looks at Psalm 23* that four things are necessary for a sheep to actually lie down.

> *"It is significant that to be at rest there must be a definite sense of freedom from fear, tension, aggravations and hunger."*

People truly are like sheep. Before my dad made us lie down on family vacations he also made it possible for us to lie down. He made sure we had a safe place to rest inside our vacation cabin and he even calmed our childhood fears by leaving the door cracked open to Mom and Dad's room guaranteeing his presence nearby. Secondly, he eased the tension between my sister and me as we shared a bed making sure we both had room, no one's feet were touching anyone else and covers were equally distributed. Next he eliminated aggravations. We all went to the potty before lying down, and he killed the annoying fly zipping overhead. Finally, Dad made sure the nap came after lunch and after that necessary drink of water.

The implication being, that like sheep, we rest more easily when our needs are met. What needs are you currently experiencing that are making it difficult for you to rest?

❀ Things I fear:

_____

_____

_____

❀ Sources of tension in my life:

_____

_____

_____

❀ Aggravating circumstances:

_____

_____

❀ Things I hunger most deeply for:

_____

_____

Your Shepherd is ready to meet your needs. His green pastures are available.

What do the following verses tell you about how your Good Shepherd is prepared to meet your needs in these four areas of concern?

1. Fear: Exodus 14:13; 2 Timothy 1:7

   _____

   _____

   _____

2. Tension: Matthew 11:29-30; 1 Peter 5:7

   _____

   _____

   _____

3. Aggravating Circumstances: Romans 5:3-5;
   2 Corinthians 4:17-18

   _____

   _____

   _____

4. Hunger: Psalm 37:25; Matthew 6:25; Luke 12:29

   _____

   _____

   _____

Which one of these truths affords you the most peace today?

_____

_____

_____

Despite the best efforts of the shepherd some sheep refuse to take advantage of the green pastures prepared for them. Literally, they think the grass is greener on the other side of the fence! Instead of lying down in rest they continue to forage about for themselves attempting to satisfy their needs on their own apart from the care of the shepherd.

Do you know any sheep like that? Don't worry. I won't ask for a show of hooves...I mean hands!

What are some of the ways you've tried to calm your own fears and meet your own needs as opposed to trusting the provision of your Shepherd?

_____

_____

_____

Green pastures alone, however, are not enough to meet a sheep's needs. Every sheep must have water.

He leads me beside quiet waters.

Have you been out to eat lately? When your pager beeps or your name is called, what happens next? "Follow me, please. Right this way. Watch your step." On through the maze of tables, people and wait staff you are led by a host whose job is to safely and productively deliver you to your destination.

It's not your responsibility to find your table. It's not even necessary for you to know where you will end up being seated. Your only assignment is to follow the leader.

Do you remember playing Follow the Leader as kids? Everyone in my neighborhood wanted to be the leader. Fights never broke out over the follower's positions, but some nasty arguments ensued in pursuit of being the leader. We all crave being in charge, don't we?

Your Shepherd longs to lead you, bring you, to quiet waters. He's leading. Are you following? Or, are you fighting Him for the Captain's seat?

When is it most difficult for you to follow God's leading?

_____

_____

_____

He leads me beside quiet waters.

As a young mother of three children aged four and under, I often felt emotionally, physically and even spiritually spent. All day long these little people needed me for just about everything. You know the sound a straw makes when you suck the last drop from the cup? Slurrrrrp. Empty. That's where I found myself.

Kurt and I were all set to enjoy a rare evening out with some other couples from church when I heard the distinct invitation of the Shepherd calling me apart to spend time with Him.

The choice lay before me—a tasty Mexican entreé or a deep, long drink of Living Water. Christian fellowship or fellowship with Christ Himself?

Kurt graciously agreed to attend the couple's night alone. Our sitter did her thing upstairs with the kids and I followed the lead of my Shepherd to His watering hole in a basement bedroom.

Several hours and one box of tissue later I emerged no longer dehydrated. My thirst had been quenched by the only One who could satisfy.

Every season of life presents its own set of challenges. At times you'll need to gulp the Living Water in order to replenish your dried-out soul. But, the best practice is to drink your fill from the quiet waters daily.

At times you'll need to gulp the Living Water in order to replenish your dried-out soul. But, the best practice is to drink your fill from the quiet waters daily.

A regular diet of green pastures and still waters eradicates panic and ensures peace.

Read Psalm 23:2 one more time. Now, close your eyes and imagine the green pastures, the quiet waters. What pictures come to mind?

_____

_____

_____

_____

_____

Put yourself in the above scene. What would it take for you to actually enjoy some quiet rest, to sit still long enough to know the sound of silence and notice that there are pastures and that they are green? How would you describe the pace of your life?

_____

_____

_____

What is keeping you from green pastures and quiet waters?

_____

_____

_____

How often are you feasting on God's Word and drinking in His promises? Have you established a regular habit of Bible Study and communing with Him in prayer?

_____

_____

_____

Vance Havener, an old southern preacher, used to say, "Come apart before you come apart." How can you carve out more time to spend with your Good Shepherd?

_____

_____

_____

❀ ❀ ❀

Let's turn Psalm 23:2 into a prayer. Will you pray with me now?

Father, thank You for making me lie down and rest even when I haven't been honest about my need for refreshment or very cooperative in slowing down. Thank You for preparing green pastures and still waters. Forgive me for the times I've rejected Your provision and sought to satisfy my needs my own way. Thank You for being my Shepherd.

Go Deep, Sheep!

Spiritual Discipline to Practice: Solitude

Scripture Passage: Mark 1:35-37

The habit of leaving other things and other people behind at certain times to be alone with the Shepherd is beneficial for a growing peace.

- ❀ Set up a specific place in your home where you will meet regularly with God. Gather your Bible, journal, Bible Study, devotional guide, pens, etc. and keep them handy in a basket or bag in your meeting place.

- ❀ Pick a day on your calendar and make a date with your Heavenly Father. Make arrangements to be alone with Him for some extra special time of communication.

- ❀ Choose a weekend to fast from socializing. Stay home and be alone with family, and as you have opportunity, alone with Jesus.

Verse to Memorize: Mark 1:35

"Very early in the morning, while it was still dark, Jesus got up, left the house and went off to a solitary place, where he prayed."

Notes

Notes

Notes

Chapter Three

Peace for Broken Places

Psalm 23:3

He restores my soul...

> "He restores it to its original purity that has now grown foul and black with sin; for alas, what good were it to have green pastures and a black soul? He restores it to its natural temper in affections, that was grown distempered with violence of passions; for alas, what good were it to have still waters and turbulent spirit? He restores it to life that has grown before in a manner quite dead."
>
> —Sir Richard Baker

I'm a flea market-aholic. The word restore speaks volumes to an antique junkie like myself. There's something terribly invigorating about rescuing a discarded piece of the past and loving it back to beauty. In essence that's what God offers to do for you and me.

Like an old table or chair that has seen better days, you and I can suffer from the bumps, bangs, and bruises of life. What are some of the things in life that cause your soul to need restoring?

> "When the soul grows sorrowful He revives it; when it is sinful He sanctifies it; when it is weak He strengthens it."
>
> —Charles Spurgeon

_____

_____

In Hebrew the word restore means, "turn back, turn around, return, movement back to the point of departure." When we sin, either knowingly or unknowingly, we depart from God's path. If we'll come to the Good Shepherd He will take our broken, sin-sick soul and turn it around.

Do you know anything about the process of restoring old furniture? What do you think has to happen to turn back the hands of time and make the piece new again?

_____

_____

_____

Scraping and sanding are most often a part of the process. Sometimes several coats of paint must be removed, rough edges smoothed and many years worth of grime and dirt scrubbed away before any real beauty can be seen.

What are some of the tools the Father has used in your life to make you ready for the restoring work He wants to accomplish in you?

_____

_____

_____

You may know first hand, as I do, how difficult it can be to endure seasons of restoration, but without the restorative process our lives remain dysfunctional wrecks.

Can you recall a specific time when God employed some radical, uncomfortable tactics to turn your life around?

_____

_____

_____

I think one of the most difficult things for parents to do is to consistently discipline their children, especially on the rare occasions when direct disobedience calls for a loving spanking. I'll never forget one time in particular with Ivy at about age four. Her exact offense has long since escaped my memory, but the prayer she prayed that day is etched in my mind forever. She squeezed her eyes shut, threw her head back and thrust both hands up into the air. "O Lord, You are my God," she cried, "and I know You don't want me to get a spanking!"

Ivy was right. I'm sure God didn't want her to have to get a spanking, but He was willing, as was I, to allow her to experience momentary pain to produce lasting good.

God's restoring work involves change. And, change is hard. It often hurts, but thankfully it's a temporary discomfort with a tremendous reward!

What do these verses teach us about the end result of God's good work in us?

Job 23:10 _____

_____

_____

Psalm 66:10 _____

_____

_____

1 Peter 1:6-7 _____

_____

_____

He restores my soul...

Combine this concept of restoration with the Hebrew definition of soul and we've just unwrapped another of God's amazing treasures!

Soul translates: "to breathe, to be refreshed, life, breath".

Look up Genesis 2:7. What happens in this verse?

_____

_____

_____

Mankind was fully alive, filled with the breath of God. Then came the fall.

Sin marked us with the kiss of death, but the Good Shepherd's restoring work breathes afresh the breath of life in us!

He restores my soul. Literally, He takes me back to the point of my sin, my departure, and refreshes me with the breath of life. Not just at salvation, but each and every time I confess, repent and seek His forgiveness God works life in me.

Look up 1 John 1:9 How confidently can we count on the restorative work of God when we confess our sin?

_____

_____

_____

Are there any sin issues that you feel convicted to confess right now?

_____

_____

_____

Are you still wondering how to trade your panic for peace? Come regularly to the Shepherd and let Him breathe life back into your being.

What are some of the areas in your life right now where you most need the restoring, healing work of God?

_____

_____

_____

Let's recap. So far in Psalm 23 we've learned that 1) the Lord is my shepherd, and 2) because He is my shepherd I don't have to live in a state of want; 3) He knows what is best for me and makes it possible for me to lie down in green pastures and drink from much needed quiet waters; 4) on our journey together He continually restores my soul. With Him I am refreshed and renewed.

Are you gaining a new sense of peace? Why not pause now to thank Him for one truth you have gleaned so far from this wonderfully rich Psalm.

_____

_____

_____

He guides me in paths of righteousness...

In 1798 an amazing discovery was made in a small Kentucky town. Thanks to John Houchins, a homesteader who shot and tracked a bear, the entrance to an entire system of underground tunnels was realized. One of the largest, Mammoth Cave, attracts numbers of tourists each year.

On a recent family outing we followed our guide deep into the dark recesses of this cave. Jagged rock formations, steep inclines followed by sharp drop-offs, twists, turns and multiple paths kept us very aware of the importance of sticking with our fearless leader. We quickly lost all sense of our present location or even which direction we were heading. Our guide, however, was a confident trailblazer, knowing the innards of the cave by heart.

Not only was our guide equipped with the knowledge of right paths inside Mammoth, but he also possessed a light. Caves are dark, as in inky black, can't-see-anything-at-all dark. The guide's light was our lifeline. Without it we were frozen in our place, paralyzed and filled with fear. With our focus fixed on our leader, however, the next step became clear.

Forrest Gump thought life was like a box of chocolates. That's sounds sweet, but in reality life is a great deal more like Mammoth Cave. The paths we travel are unpredictable and uncertain at best; down right treacherous at worst. That is enough to rob the average traveler of any sense of peace.

How can we proceed without panic when we don't even know which way to turn? Who will be our guide? Who will shine the light on our darkest days?

He guides me in paths of righteousness...

Your Shepherd has offered to guide you in right paths; paths of righteousness, literally, the paths that ought to be.

What current situation in your life has you searching for God's guidance?

_____

_____

_____

How can you determine if you are walking the right path? Look up Psalm 119:105 and Proverbs 16:9.

_____

_____

_____

Phillip Keller gives us even more insight into our need for a guide when he describes the habits of sheep.

> *"Sheep are notorious creatures of habit. If left to themselves they will follow the same trails until they become ruts; graze the same hills until they turn to desert wastes; pollute their own ground until it is corrupt with disease and parasites."*

The Shepherd's guidance not only delivers a sense of safety and direction, but it also creates an environment of health and vitality.

Can you identify any destructive habits in your life that need to be placed under the guidance of your Shepherd?

_____

_____

_____

All of these benefits, protection, direction and care, are available to sheep belonging to a conscientious shepherd. Can you see how important it is to make sure you have the right guide?

The Shepherd's guidance not only delivers a sense of safety and direction, but it also creates an environment of health and vitality.

Want-a-be guides abound. From Dr. Phil and Oprah to your well-meaning mother-in-law, you are bombarded daily by those who attempt to tell you what to think, what to believe and how to live. Millions of advertising dollars are invested to generate a following for products and services guaranteed to improve your journey. To whom will you choose to listen?

Who or what are some of the guides competing for your allegiance?

_____

_____

_____

One morning my house was unusually quiet. The other children were already off to school, but my three year old, Ellie, remained at large. Silence may be golden in some instances, but not when a toddler is on the loose! I left my bedroom to search and had only made it around the corner to the top of the stairs when I heard a little voice.

Ellie was sitting on her bottom scooting backwards up the stairs while attempting to bring a very large stool with her. With every step she repeated the same phrase, "I just need a wittle bit of help. I just need a wittle bit of help."

When it comes to knowing who to follow we each need at least a wittle bit of help. Sometimes we need a whole lot of help!

In days of old, travelers would hire a guide to help them navigate unfamiliar terrain in route to their destination. Read what the *Evangelical Commentary on the Bible* has to say about the selection of a guide.

> *"The professional guides' name or reputation was the traveler's only guarantee of protection and safe arrival."*

Because the guide assumes responsibility for the followers, his entire reputation is at stake. His name is on the line.

David says,

He guides me in paths of righteousness for His Name's sake.

A name is a word used to identify a person. I am identified by the name Kristen even though legally I am Anna Kristen. In the south calling a child by a middle name is common practice. When I was very young my mother would occasionally refer to me as Krissy. My maiden name was McColl and my married name is Sauder, so if you add up all my monikers, I actually have five.

It takes a handful of names to identify this little lamb, but to describe The Shepherd, well He's indescribable! Our feeble attempts to grasp all of Who He really is have required so many names that Scripture is literally full of Names of God.

Read through this sampling of the Names of the Lord and then find a verse in Psalm 23 that highlights each particular characteristic.

Jehovah–Rohi, God the Shepherd

_____

_____

Jehovah–Jirah, The Lord My Provider

_____

_____

Jehovah–Shalom, The Lord My Peace

_____

_____

Jehovah–Rophi, The Lord Who Heals

_____

_____

Jehovah–Tsidkenu, The Lord Our Righteousness

_____

_____

Jehovah–Shammah, The Lord is There

_____

_____

Based on these few Names of the Lord what kind of guide do you think God will be for you?

_____

_____

Why is it important that He is leading us "for His Name's sake"? What do you think this means?

_____

_____

Dear Lord, My soul is often weary and beaten down by life. I confess that I need Your restoring work to make me whole and give me peace. Help me walk in the righteous path You put before me. In Jesus' Name, Amen.

Go Deep, Sheep!

Spiritual Discipline to Practice: Silence

Scripture Passage: Lamentations 3:25-26

My dad used to say, "It's so loud in here I can't hear myself think!" Life screams for our attention competing with the Spirit's whisper.

- ❀ Use a journal and pen to write down what you hear God saying to you in your quiet times with Him.

- ❀ Take a walk and listen to the sounds of the Creator all around.

- ❀ Fast from noise! Set aside a day to try life without TV, radio, telephone, cell phone or any other artificial sounds.

Verse to Memorize: Lamentations 3:26
"It is good to wait quietly for the salvation of the Lord."

Notes

· ·

Notes

Chapter Four

Peace in the Shadows

Psalm 23:4

Even though I walk through the valley of the shadow of death, I will fear no evil, for you are with me; your rod and your staff, they comfort me.

> *Notwithstanding, while we are herein this life, he feeds us with the sweet pastures of the wholesome herbs of his holy word, until we come to eternal life; and when we put off these bodies, and come into heaven, and know the blessed fruition and riches of his kingdom, then shall we not only be his sheep, but also the guests of his everlasting banquet; which, Lord thou settest before all them that love thee in this world, and dost so anoint and make glad our minds with thine Holy Spirit; that no adversities nor troubles can make us sorry."*
>
> *~ John Hooper (martyr) 1495-1555*

There are so many treasures packed into this one verse. I just want to rip it open like a kid at Christmas. But sometimes when you tear into a gift too quickly you miss something.

Has that ever happened at your house? The giver calls out, "Wait! There's more," and you lift the tissue paper to reveal a special something that would have gone unnoticed. We don't want to overlook anything God desires to give us in Psalm 23:4, so we're just going to have to restrain ourselves and proceed slowly.

Because each word is a powerhouse of truth, we'll start at the very beginning.

Even though...

Suffering is inevitable. Hardships and tragedies find us all. They are no respecter of persons. At times we become angry with God because of the difficult circumstances He allows, but He has been honest with us about pain's reality.

Look up John 16:33 and copy it on the lines provided.

_____

_____

_____

David doesn't say, "If I walk through the valley." He says, "even though." Count on valley experiences. Life's pathway runs through the valleys. If you're not in one now, you will be at some point in the future. Chances are you've already crossed a few.

What are some of the valleys you've already faced?

_____

_____

_____

Even though I walk through the valley of the shadow of death...

If you've ever watched Disney's Snow White you'll probably remember the scene where the woodsman abandons the young beauty in the forest. The deeper she ventures under the treed canopy the more scraggly the limbs appear. Eerie squawks and shrill sounds echo from behind bushes. Snow White grows fearful, picking up the pace she glances over her shoulder and then breaks into a run.

Have you ever been scared, really scared? There's something about fear that makes a body want to move fast. The adrenaline rushes. All systems are go and we shift into overdrive.

It's not normal to walk through a valley, especially one named The Valley of the Shadow of Death! So it is in life. When tough times assail it's our natural tendency to want to pass through them quickly. Yet David identifies his pace as a walk.

> Trips through valleys are not meaningless treks. A valley is the best passageway to reach a bountiful destination.

How do you think David was able to walk through the valley?

_____

_____

_____

It all comes back to the guide, doesn't it? A good shepherd knows what's on the other side of the valley, and he under-stands that for the well being of the sheep, they must pass that way. If sheep trust their shepherd they won't bolt when he leads them to higher ground and better pasture by valley's trail.

Trips through valleys are not meaningless treks. A valley is the best passageway to reach a bountiful destination.

Phillip Keller describes three benefits to the valley path. Let me summarize them for you:

1) Because the sheep are on the move they are alone in the presence of the shepherd to an even more intimate degree than when in home pastures.

2) Valleys provide the best source of water during transit.

3) Valleys offer the best feed en route to higher ground.

God never wastes a valley experience. What are some lessons you have learned in your valley days?

_____

_____

_____

Even though I walk __through__ the valley of the shadow of death...

Through is an encouraging word as it pertains to valleys. Aren't you thrilled to know that David made it to the other side! He came out of the valley, and you will too.

David securely asserts,

Even though I walk through the valley of the shadow of death, __I will fear no evil__...

What are some of the evils you fear in this life? Do you think it is possible to live fear free?

_____

_____

_____

One of my besetting sins is worry. From migraine headaches to fever blisters, even when I'm not consciously anxious, my body sends signals of inner unrest. Thankfully, I've traded much of my panic for peace over the years as God's Spirit keeps overhauling me from the inside out. My husband serves as a tool in the Spirit's hands. Kurt will often say to me, "Kristen, what is the worst that can happen?"

That question pops things into perspective. For a Christ follower there is no worst that can happen. Death just equals more life, and a better one at that!

The truth is, there is NO cause for panic if the Lord is your shepherd. Erwin McManus wrote in Uprising,

> *"Freedom comes not by avoiding pain and suffering, nor by prolonging our existence, but through the freedom from fear and the confidence that not even death can rob us of life."*

Even though I walk through the valley of the shadow of death...

Well-known passages like Psalm 23 are often read with a familiarity that obscures finer details. For example, have you ever paid attention to the word shadow in Psalm 23:4? We should not overlook the fact that the valley is not called Death, but The Shadow of Death.

Why do you think that might be important?

_____

_____

_____

The Hebrew phrase "shadow of death" translates in English to include shadow, darkness, gloom and blackness. There is a great deal of darkness, even mystery surrounding death. It's not like we get to practice so that the second or sequential times will become easier.

Part of our fear comes from the unknown. I remember giving birth for the first time. Because my water was leaking I was admitted to the hospital before experiencing even one contraction. I had naively settled into my birthing room when I heard anguished screams nearby.

> "Freedom comes not by avoiding pain and suffering, nor by prolonging our existence, but through the freedom from fear and the confidence that not even death can rob us of life."
> ~Erwin McManus

Every muscle in my body tensed. "Is she having a baby?" I asked. When the nurse responded in the affirmative I began to wonder what in the world I had gotten myself into! Not that childbirth is ever a piece of cake, but having babies two, three and four were less intense simply because I knew what to expect.

Familiar territory helps. However, there is nothing familiar about death. Everyone dies only once so, no one knows exactly what it will be like.

But I do know this; there is a big difference between a shadow of a thing and the thing itself. A small animal can make a fairly large shadow in the right light. Even non-threatening objects cast some pretty spooky images at certain angles!

The shadow of an alarm clock on a bedroom wall may realistically resemble a monster's head with antennas. The shadow may cause you to look twice, but as soon as you realize it's just an alarm clock your fear subsides. You might even feel kind of silly for being frightened at all.

In a similar way, the shadow of death lays out an intimidating form, but when we understand that Christ has conquered death, that death is not this huge, heinous enemy, we can say with the Apostle Paul the words he wrote in Philippians 1:21.

Look up the verse and write it in your own words:

_____

_____

_____

I will fear no evil, for you are with me...

If you were facing a valley who would you most want to walk through it with you?

_____

_____

_____

Here is one of the best reasons you have for trading your panic for peace; your Shepherd is with you!

He is with you in the green pastures.
He is with you by quiet waters.
He is with you on right paths.
He is with you in the valleys.

your rod and your staff, they comfort me...

Well-worn sweaters, bubble baths, mac-n-cheese and chocolate, we use many things to bring comfort to our lives. What are some of the things you turn to for comfort?

_____

_____

_____

_____

What does God's comfort look like in your life?

_____

_____

_____

_____

Rods and staffs aren't typical objects of comfort, but in the hand of a caring shepherd they speak love.

David would have used the curve of his staff to draw a particular sheep to himself or to tenderly pull a sheep onto a right path correcting his erring way. With his rod, David counted the flock, like a mother in a mall tapping each child on the head before proceeding to make sure she hasn't lost one.

Read Luke 15:3-6. What did this shepherd do when after counting his sheep one turned up missing?

_____

_____

_____

Ivy was our little one who loved to be carried. My arms were regularly busy holding baby Ellie or lugging diaper bags so, many times, Ivy was forced to walk. But, it wasn't the free ride she was really after anyway. Ivy craved contact. Touch to her spelled comfort. On the occasions when my arms were full she would ask, "Mommy, will you carry my hand?"

The Good Shepherd counted His sheep, (possibly using His rod), discovered one missing, searched until He found it, and then carried the lamb home.

Can you think of a situation in your life when Christ has "carried" you?

_____

_____

_____

Have you ever tried to carry a squirming toddler who is doing every thing in his power to escape your loving arms? That's not an easy job!

Sometimes you and I resist God's offer to carry us. We thrash and pull against His strong arms feeling confined by His restraining grasp. Do you have a situation in your life right now that you need to surrender to the Father's firm grip?

_____

_____

_____

Read Psalm 46:10 and write the verse in your own words below.

_____

_____

_____

"Be still," the Psalmist says. Literally this phrase commands "cease striving". What would it take for you to stop fighting against the Lord and simply collapse in His embrace?

_____

_____

_____

A shepherd's rod has other uses that comfort his sheep as well. The rod can be hurled at a predator demonstrating the shepherd's role as protector. It can be used to part thick sheep's wool to examine the animal for cleanliness, health and proper growth.

In another Psalm David authored he invites the examination of his Good Shepherd,

Search me, O God, and know my heart; test me and know my anxious thoughts. See if there is any offensive way in me, and lead me in the way everlasting. ~Psalm 139:23-24

Panic is a peculiar thing. It can lay in hiding under the surface of our lives waiting to erupt like a crop of teenage acne. As if we're riding a roller coaster at an amusement park, we enjoy seasons of peace but know the next big drop is somewhere up ahead.

For some of us panic is not so sporadic. It has become a constant, taking up residency in our lives, leaving us to cope daily with the current of unrest churning and gnawing at our insides.

We've talked throughout this study about some of the BIG panic buttons, like death, unsettling world events, dealing with our past, etc. These can certainly rob us of peace, but let's not overlook everyday frustrations as probable peace nabbers.

> *For some of us panic is not so sporadic. It has become a constant, taking up residency in our lives, leaving us to cope daily with the current of unrest churning and gnawing at our insides.*

As Dick Sattler says, "Life is just so daily." It's the ordinary stuff, the chores, the bills, the job, difficult relationships, long "to do" lists, allergies, whining kids, unrealistic expectations, and on and on that have this sheep bleating about what a baaaa-d day it's been.

What about you? What are the little irritations that try to steal your peace on a regular basis?

_____

_____

_____

My mother used to have a sign on her desk that read, "I finally got it all together, but I forgot where I put it!"

Can you relate? I sure can. It takes a ton of energy to look put together on the outside when your insides are frazzled.

We might be able to keep our lack of peace hidden from others, but there's no way, sister sheep, to "pull the wool" over God's eyes! He knows the truth.

Why not follow David's example and invite your Shepherd to use His staff to draw you near and His rod of comfort to part the wool of your heart and give you a good once-over today?

Read again Psalm 139: 23-24 then use this space to write your own prayer asking God to search you, pointing out any anxious thoughts or offensive ways.

_____

_____

_____

Why not talk to the Father now? Make this prayer your own.

Dear Father, What a Good Shepherd You are and how blessed I am to be Yours! I have so much to thank You for after studying Psalm 23:4. Thank You, Jesus, that You have conquered death. I have nothing to fear. Thank You that You will never leave me to walk my valleys alone. You are with me always. Thank You for the comfort of Your rod and staff. Even when it's difficult to hold still under Your inspection, help me to cease striving and know You are God. I surrender now my daily worries and confess them as sin, trading them for Your peace. In Jesus Name I pray. Amen.

Spiritual Discipline to Practice: Prayer

Scripture Passage: Ephesians 6:18; Philippians 4:6-7

D.L. Moody said, "A day without prayer is a boast against God." Start your day, fill your day, and end your day in communication with the Shepherd of Peace.

- ❦ Begin your day by putting on the armor of God. Pray through each piece listed in Ephesians 6:13-17.
- ❦ Take a prayer walk and talk to the Lord about specific valleys you face.
- ❦ Fast, just for today, from calling mom, sister, or girlfriends for help and direct all your SOS calls to God Himself. Pay attention to how He answers.
- ❦ Kneel beside your bed before you climb in and thank your Shepherd for always being with you.

Verse to Memorize: Ephesians 6:18a
"And pray in the Spirit on all occasions with all kinds of prayers and requests."

Notes

Notes

Chapter Five
Peace from
Abundant Provision

Psalm 23:5

You prepare a __table__ before me...

At the right time of the year a shepherd herds his flock up to high elevations to graze. In the west these pristine pastures are known by their Spanish name, mesa, meaning table. Scouting out watering holes, adding salt blocks and essential minerals in specific locations, and in general becoming familiar with the lay of the land, the shepherd literally prepares these table lands in advance for his sheep.

Can you relate to this busy shepherd as he hustles to make his "table" ready for a crowd?

At the reading of this verse my mind drifts back to all the tables I've readied over the years. From tea parties for teddies set with plastic dishes, to paper plates and streamers at birthday parties, to Grandma's fine china on Thanksgiving Day, there have been quite a few tables prepared.

It's a simple pleasure really, born of necessity. The table has to be set so we can eat. Yet, for those of us who enjoy the job it becomes an artistic expression of love for family and friends mixed with the joy celebrations bring.

Think back to some of the tables you have prepared. What was the process? What went into getting that table ready?

_____

_____

_____

Some women are natural hosts. It's just their thing. They don't stress out when company's coming. Meals flow together effortlessly. Decorating, cleaning, and in general making their home guest-ready is invigorating not depleting. Then there are the rest of us.

The story is told about a family holding a special dinner. The mother, anxious to make a good impression, enlisted the help of husband and children. Everyone scurried about at a frantic pace until the guests arrived and all were seated for the meal. As they bowed their heads to say grace the mother called upon the little girl to offer up thanks. The daughter, however, was not sure what to say. "Just say what I would say," her mother instructed. So she bowed her head and stated clearly, "Dear Lord, why in the world did I invite all these people over here today!"

Entertaining is often a quick way to start the panic waters rising. What is it about having people over that puts many of us over the edge?

When you read Psalm 23:5 what picture of God comes to mind as He prepares His table?

_____

_____

It is impossible to even pretend God was rushed, anxious, insecure or irritable in His preparations. And, when the host is calm, cool and collected, the guests are put at rest.

I've attended a few genuinely posh dinners in my lifetime, but they aren't my favorite. Don't misunderstand. I'm a girly-girl, as my daughters would say, but formal events are just so...formal! Between sucking your tummy flat, keeping your bra strap from peeking out from under the little black dress, and being careful not to dribble anything on your dry-clean-only attire, how's a lady to relax?

Many of us worry about getting everything just right for company. We stress out and hand our peace to the enemy on a silver platter. We forget that guests feel most appreciated and cared for, not when the meal is gourmet and the décor is designer, but when we're calm enough to enjoy meaningful relationships.

How are you doing with hospitality? Read Romans 12:13, Hebrews 13:2, and 1 Peter 4:9. Write a summary of Jesus' instructions in your own words.

_____

_____

_____

What can you do to trade some of your everything's-got-to-be-perfect panic into the peace that your Shepherd demonstrates as He prepares a table in Psalm 23:5?

_____

_____

_____

Recently, our two youngest girls, Ivy and Ellie, were a part of the same ballet recital. After two trips downtown for dress rehearsal and performance along with all that goes into getting two tiny ballerinas ready for the stage, we were all completely worn out. To celebrate, Kurt offered to skip the original, less expensive plan of having everyone over for a home cooked meal, and instead take the entire bunch out for dinner.

Out of all possible options, the girls picked fast food! Sufficiently filled and relaxed we climbed back into the van. I smiled at Kurt and said, "Hamburger—99 cents, frosty—99 cents, not having to cook or clean the kitchen," Kurt chimed in with me, "Priceless!"

There's so much behind the scenes work that goes into preparing a table. As Christians we can easily forget all that Christ, our Shepherd, endured to prepare a table on our behalf. The Lord's Table, communion with the Father, was made ready at the highest cost to Christ.

As a fourth grade child I memorized Isaiah 53, the prophetic passage describing Christ's sacrificial death to bring us to God. It pierces my heart to this day. Turn in your Bible now and ponder this chapter writing down your observations about all Christ did to prepare the table of communion for us.

_____

_____

_____

You prepare a table before me...

By emphasizing the phrase "before me" we uncover another lesson that will enable us to trade panic for peace. For whom is the Shepherd's table being prepared?

_____

_____

_____

For you, little lamb, for you! The Shepherd is laying out a spread and you're the guest of honor. Just as David the shepherd led his flock to graze on higher ground, your Shepherd has prepared an elevated plane of living for you. He longs for you to rise above the daily worries, concerns and sins that so easily weight you down. Won't you accept His invitation and come to Him?

Take this opportunity to RSVP to your Shepherd's invitation. How does it make you feel to be His honored guest? What would you like to say to Him now?

_____

_____

_____

_____

_____

_____

_____

_____

> ...your Shepherd has prepared an elevated plane of living for you. He longs for you to rise above the daily worries, concerns and sins that so easily weight you down.

What kind of menu has the Shepherd lined up for this occasion, delightful delicacies or low-fat fare? Read Psalm 37:3-4 to discover some of what the Lord has planned to give us.

_____

_____

_____

When we delight ourselves in the Good Shepherd He gives us the desires of our heart. Do you think that includes chocolate?

At one and a half years of age our oldest daughter Olivia turned up missing. Frantically I called for her, searching every inch of the house. At long last I discovered Livie hiding behind the living room sofa with cheeks stuffed full of candy, melting goo oozing down her chin rolls and dripping onto her white onesie. One fist grasped the almost empty incriminating bag. Her other hand shoved the remaining chocolate pieces into her face at lightning speed hoping to get every last one before I could stop her.

Yes, His table includes dishes we desire, but like any caregiver, His plate is also laden with all things good and beneficial, whether we'd choose them or not.

In researching the habits of sheep for this study I wasn't surprised to learn that the furry little creatures will munch on just about anything in their path, even things that would be better left alone. Table lands, while lush with the greenest of grasses may also contain poisonous weeds and blossoms. A good shepherd remains vigilant about ridding the "table" of harmful substances. His desire is for the sheep to partake of all the good he sets before them, not the potentially hurtful things they're drawn to on their own.

What are some of the potentially harmful things you find yourself attracted to in this life?

_____

_____

_____

Have you ever chomped a children's chewable vitamin? Don't! My kids have attempted all manor of deception to avoid their daily dose of taste bud torture. I've extracted them from balled up napkins, slid them from beneath breakfast plate rims and rescued one from the trash can. While I sympathize with my children's displeasure I still require vitamin consumption because it's what's best for growing bodies.

And so it is with God's love, we will at times find His table set with character inducing suffering or with trials that produce perseverance. But, we can be sure that everything we find there is good for us and for our growth.

The rule in the Sauder home is you don't plop down at the table and complain about the meal mom's prepared. You try a little bite of everything that's served. It's not a restaurant. The one who fixes the meal determines the menu.

Maybe you've been grazing on God's good provisions while nurturing a bad attitude. Could it be that part of your lack of peace stems from a desire to have a God who will give you whatever you want? When He serves up something you're not wild about how do you respond?

_____

_____

_____

Is there anything on your plate at the moment that you're having trouble swallowing?

_____

_____

_____

> *Your Shepherd is holding a banquet just for you. Come feast on His promises and find peace!*

Just like my kids and their vitamins, the temptation is to push away what God offers and fill up on all the junk we scavenge on our own. If your plate's too full you may need to look closely at the contents. Maybe some of what you're currently munching on is not from the Shepherd at all.

What stressful situations have you piled onto your own plate that could be eliminated?

_____

_____

_____

Don't stubbornly sit alone eating the PBJ (Panicked Busyness Jumble) you made for yourself. Your Shepherd is holding a banquet just for you. Come feast on His promises and find peace!

You prepare a table before me <u>in the presence of my enemies</u>...

Define enemy.

_____

_____

We've all heard it said, "She's her own worst enemy." Who and/or what are your enemies?

_____

_____

David, the author of Psalm 23 certainly knew about enemies. He tangled with foes both as a shepherd and as a King. David the shepherd fought off dangerous predators to protect the life of his sheep. Look up 1 Samuel 17:36. What enemies had David killed to save his flock?

_____

_____

Can you imagine the terror a ewe must experience when a lion roars nearby? She's a bleating ball of yarn. What's she going to do to stop her attacker? Scream, "Get Baaa-k"? The point is she's helpless, completely unable to defend herself. Apart from the shepherd, she's lamb chops for sure.

Read the description of the Christian's enemy in 1 Peter 5:8 and jot down what you learn.

_____

_____

> *"As host, God assures us of welcome at his rich table, of abundance, attendance, and unending hospitality. All this even now, while enemies surround us."*
> ~Evangelical Commentary on the Bible

Let's make sure we get this straight. The Bible depicts us as sheep and our enemy, the devil, as a lion on the prowl. What's to keep us from becoming lamb chops spiritually speaking?

_____

_____

_____

_____

If you answered, "The Shepherd," you're catching on quick! The Lord is our provider and protector. This entire Psalm details His tender care for us, His sheep. Even as we feast at the table He has prepared before us He remains alert, aware of the enemy's presence.

> *"As host, God assures us of welcome at his rich table, of abundance, attendance, and unending hospitality. All this even now, while enemies surround us." (Evangelical Commentary on the Bible)*

As Christians, how important is it for us to be aware of our enemy? Consider these verses: 1 Peter 5:8, and James 4:7.

_____

_____

_____

_____

How does the reality of a spiritual enemy impact your peace on a daily basis?

_____

_____

_____

_____

Under attack, sheep have been known to remain completely quiet. Basically, they're scared silent. Have you ever experienced one of those nightmares where you want to scream, you're trying to scream, but nothing comes out? Well, that's the story for sheep in crisis.

Phillip Keller in a Shepherd Looks at the 23rd Psalm reminds us that this can be our story too:

> "The same is true of Christians. Many of us get into deep difficulty beyond ourselves; we are stricken dumb with apprehension, unable even to call or cry out for help; we just crumple under our adversary's attack."

It pays to stay close to the Shepherd. By drawing near to him even our faintest cry commands His immediate attention.

Read the first three verses of Psalm 40. See if you can find two things that David does and six actions that the Lord takes on David's behalf.

David   1) _____

             2) _____

The Lord 1) _____

           2) _____

           3) _____

           4) _____

           5) _____

           6) _____

When we cry out to the Lord and wait patiently for Him He will turn to us and hear our cry for help. He will lift us out of the slimy pits we plunge into (or climb into!). He will set our feet on a rock, give us a firm place to stand and put a new song of praise in our mouth.

What is keeping you from living the "high life" the Shepherd has prepared for you on His table lands?

_____

_____

_____

How can you draw near to the Lord?

_____

_____

_____

What are some of the habits or spiritual disciplines that you have found helpful in developing your personal relationship with the Savior?

_____

_____

You _anoint_ my head with oil.

Olive oil, so important in the Jewish culture, was often used in special ceremonies as a sign of gladness. Look up the following Scriptures and record the occasion that called for an anointing with oil in each.

1 Samuel 10:1 _____

_____

_____

2 Kings 9:3, 6 _____

_____

_____

A King was anointed to demonstrate that he was called out and set apart. In Eastern tradition distinguished guests were often anointed with perfumed oil in an act of great respect.

T.C. Barth comments, "In the East no entertainment could be without this, and it served, as elsewhere a bath does, for bodily refreshment. Here, however, it is naturally to be understood of the spiritual oil of gladness."

Nathanael Hardy adds, "Anointing the head with oil is great refreshment. There are three qualities of oil—a smoothness to the touch, brightness to the sight, fragrancy to the smell, and so, gratifying the senses, it must needs cause delight to those anointed with it."

This symbolism may be a stretch for us, girls. Most of us grew up in a culture that frowns upon an oily head. We shower and shampoo daily consuming products by the squirt-fulls that promise oil free follicles. But in David's day anyone with their head anointed would have been excited to model the shiny look. It was an honor.

Anointing the head with oil was often times one part of a larger celebration including a feast.

Look back at Psalm 23:5. Write out the phrase that comes before *you anoint my head with oil.*

_____

_____

_____

Now, write out the phrase that follows *you anoint my head with oil.*

_____

_____

_____

All of these phrases together point to the Shepherd as host presiding over a lavish banquet in celebration of His chosen guest of honor.

When I was in seventh grade my classmates elected me as the representative for homecoming court. This honor came as quite a shock. I struggled believing they actually chose me and secretly ran through my mental list of more popular, outgoing and beautiful girls in our grade who were obviously better fits. Feeling like an imposter I attended the meetings set up to organize homecoming night all the while certain that someone would realize I didn't belong and send me back to class!

Maybe all this extravagant talk about banquets in your honor and being chosen by God has you thinking there must be some mistake. Are you more comfortable working hard to please God than you are reclining as His favored guest? Do you sometimes feel insignificant, unimportant, overlooked and underappreciated?

Look up the following Scriptures that emphasize how precious you are to your Heavenly Father. What can you learn from them today?

Matthew 6:26 _____

_____

_____

Matthew 10:29-31 _____

_____

_____

You anoint my head with oil.

There's another wonderful application to Psalm 23:5...*you anoint my head with oil,* that is understood through the relationship of sheep to shepherd.

Sheep can be terribly bothered by the nasal fly that is attracted to the moist membranes of the sheep's nose as the perfect place for laying their eggs. Once in place, the eggs hatch and the worm-like larvae travel up the nasal passages into the sheep's head causing a great deal of infection. Gross!

This is where the oil comes into play. A good shepherd will "anoint" the sheep's head with an oil-based repellent to keep those pesky flies at bay. Sheep who lack this protective antidote will actually beat their heads against trees, roll around on the ground in misery, pace frantically or run madly about in an attempt to rid themselves of the annoyance. Some have been known to wear themselves out even to the point of death.

Amazing how tiny flies can cause such a ruckus. Yet, I have to admit, it's so often the little things in life that get under my skin and start me stomping. Not being able to get a live voice on the phone, dropping my purse in the rain, stubbing my toe, running late to a meeting, losing my keys, burning the bake sale cookies—small aggravations that add up to a swarm of trouble for my attitude.

Any day of the week is open season for all of these irritants that fly in the face of my peace. I need an oil bath to settle me down.

Throughout the Bible oil is symbolic of the Holy Spirit. Take note of what these verses teach:

Acts 2:1-4 _____

_____

_____

1 John 2:20, 27 _____

_____

_____

Listen to how Phillip Keller describes the difference in the sheep when the oil is in place.

> "Once the oil had been applied to the sheep's head there was an immediate change in behavior. Gone was the aggravation; gone the frenzy; gone the irritability and the restlessness. Instead, the sheep would start to feed quietly again, then soon lie down in peaceful contentment."

Anoint in the Hebrew literally means: to thrive, grow fat, to anoint, give health; to remove the ashes; to prosper, be satisfied, be soaked; to be covered with fat.

In essence He says to you, His little lamb, "I want you to thrive, to grow fat spiritually speaking, to be full of emotional heath and wholeness. Don't wallow in the ashes of mourning and discouragement. I long to see you prosper and be satisfied with all that I offer you."

It's only when we live our lives moment by moment filled with the Holy Spirit that we enjoy peaceful contentment in spite of inevitable, daily frustrations. Take a moment now to express your appreciation for the Shepherd's anointing oil and even ask Him for a fresh application for your life today.

_____

_____

_____

_____

_____

_____

> *It's only when we live our lives moment by moment filled with the Holy Spirit that we enjoy peaceful contentment in spite of inevitable, daily frustrations.*

Up until this point in the Psalm David has focused on all the things the Shepherd does for His sheep.

- ❀ making you lie down in green pastures,
- ❀ leading you beside quiet waters,
- ❀ restoring your soul,
- ❀ guiding you in right paths,
- ❀ walking with you through the valleys,
- ❀ comforting you with His rod and staff,
- ❀ preparing a table full of all good things before you,
- ❀ keeping watch for the enemy, and finally
- ❀ anointing your head with oil.

Unable to contain his gratitude any longer David cries out, *my cup overflows!*

My cup overflows...

Recently our ten year-old son, Drew, has become enamored with the combustible properties of carbonation in a can. In other words, he gets a kick out of shaking our soda so that when we pop the top it erupts! He laughs his heart out watching a sister jump away from spewing bubbles.

Of course I scold him, not just for aggravating his siblings, but also for the waste. I'm careful to keep all liquids contained. I don't want to spill a drop. That's exactly the opposite of the sentiment expressed in Psalm 23:5. In this verse David is most likely demonstrating the influence of an old Eastern tradition.

"In the East the people frequently anoint their visitors with some very fragrant perfume; and give them a cup or glass of some choice wine, which they are careful to fill till it runs over. The first was designed to show their love and respect; the latter to imply that while they remained there, they should have an abundance of everything." Samuel Burder

One writer in the early 1800's says, *"Thou hast not confined thy bounty merely to the necessaries of life, but thou hast supplied me also with its luxuries."*

What does Jesus say about this concept of abundance in John 10:10?

_____

_____

_____

Christ came that we might have life and that we might have it to overflowing. He longs to fill you up with so much of His goodness that your one little life won't be able to contain it all. You will behave like a can of cola in a child's hands. Then your bounty will run over into the lives of those around you.

Who would you like to see benefit from the overflow of God's goodness in your life? Family, friends, neighbors? Make a short, specific list here and ask God to use you to influence them with His love.

_____

_____

_____

_____

Never forget, dear sister sheep, that our cups are not filled without a price. David cried out with thanksgiving for a cup that overflowed; our Savior cried out to the Father in regards to His cup as well. Read Matthew 26:38-39, 42. To what cup is Christ referring?

_____

_____

_____

Jesus, our Lord, held the cup of suffering and death and beseeched His Father for some other way. There was none. If our cups were to be filled to overflowing He had to drink His until it was empty. And so, He humbled Himself and became obedient to death, even death on a cross, Philippians 2:8.

Jesus lives to pour His fullness into our uplifted cups.

His cup was full when ours was empty. He drank His, emptying it completely. Now He lives to pour His fullness into our uplifted cups. Yet our cups can never hold all of His fullness at once, so He continues to fill us daily causing our cups to constantly run over. When we live and love others out of this overflow we trade panic for peace!

How would you describe overflow living?

_____

_____

_____

What is the opposite of overflow living?

_____

_____

What do you think it would take for you to keep your life
under His stream and live from a full cup?

_____

_____

_____

Read John 5:2-6. What did Jesus ask this man?

_____

_____

_____

At first glance that may seem like a strange, even ridiculous,
question. What sick person wouldn't want to be healed?
Still, I've met a few people in my lifetime who have grown
comfortable with their unhealthy condition. At least they
find it familiar. Besides, getting well can require work,
exercise, proper nutrition, taking the advice of someone else,
and even the expense of medication. And what would
happen to the sympathy and attention they're getting from
others? Jesus asked, "Do you want to get well?"

I have a similar question for you today. Do you want to be
filled?

Last month I experienced for the umpteenth time in my life every woman's favorite appointment—my yearly gynecological exam. Do all Doctors make small talk before they slide the stirrups into place? Mine does. I'm guessing it's a futile attempt to help the female patient relax. Anyway, he asked what I had been doing recently for fun. I told him I was in the middle of writing a Bible Study, Trading Panic for Peace.

"Wow," he replied, "That's certainly a needed topic." He went on to explain how he treats an ever-increasing number of women for anxiety disorders ranging from mild to severe. That didn't sound too surprising to me. However, his next statement grabbed my attention. "In our culture today, I'm just not sure we're willing to make the changes we need to make to live peace-filled lives."

Ladies, we can do a great deal of moaning about the absence of peace in our lives, but are we willing to do what we need to do to gain a life of tranquility? It's been said that a person will stay the same until the pain of staying the same is greater than the pain of change.

- ❀ You may need to admit that anxiety is not a personality trait; it's sin.

- ❀ It may be time to trade minutes on the phone complaining to a girlfriend for time on your knees crying out to God.

- ❀ Possibly your pace and priorities will need readjusting so that time alone with Jesus can become a reality instead of just wishful thinking.

Is the Holy Spirit bringing anything to mind that needs to change in order for you to know His peace?

_____

_____

_____

_____

Your Shepherd is ready to fill your cup to overflowing. Why not make the words of this hymn by Richard Blanchard your own?

> *"Like the woman at the well I was searching for things that could not satisfy, until I heard my Savior speaking, 'Draw from my well that never shall run dry.'*
>
> *Fill my cup, Lord. I lift it up, Lord.*
> *Come and quench this thirsting of my soul.*
> *Bread of heaven, feed me till I want no more,*
> *Fill my cup. Fill it up and make me whole."*

Pray with me,

Dear Jesus, thank You for being willing to drink the cup of suffering so that my bone-dry soul can be filled. I want the life of abundance that your death in my place made possible and I am ready to make changes that will move me toward a life of peace. I lift my cup to You and humbly receive Your anointing.

Spiritual Discipline to Practice: Gratitude

Scripture Passage: 1 Thessalonians 5:16-18

Haven't we all heard that it takes more muscles to frown than to smile! Turn that frown upside down and develop an attitude of gratitude.

- ❀ Keep a running "Thankful List." Add to it each night before bed.

- ❀ Write a thank you note to someone God has used to impact your life.

- ❀ Set aside one day to fast from asking God for anything. Instead spend your time thanking Him for all the things He does for you that you usually take for granted.

Verse to Memorize: I Thessalonians 5:16-18
"Be joyful always; pray continually; give thanks in all circumstances, for this is God's will for you in Christ Jesus."

Notes

Notes

Chapter Six
Peace in Practice

Psalm 23:6

Surely goodness and lovingkindness will follow me all the days of my life... NASB

Goodness, literally all that is good and desirable, and lovingkindness, in the Hebrew hesed, loyal, unfailing love, devotion and kindness, will follow me. When I'm resting in green pastures God's goodness and lovingkindness will be there. Yes, even through the valley, where enemies surround, and on up to the tableland, goodness and love will be with me because my Shepherd is with me.

One of the biggest adjustments of motherhood for me was getting used to being followed. Literally everywhere I went some little person went with me, clinging to my leg, climbing in my lap. Even my morning shower, on the days I got one, was punctuated by the cold shot of yesterday's bath water as a chubby toddler fist squeezed rubber ducky in my direction. Bathroom, bedroom, kitchen, laundry—it didn't matter. Where I went there they went also.

The tenacity of a two year-old to be where mommy is paints a picture for us of our inability to shake God's goodness and love. There's nothing you can do, little lamb, to make Him retreat. He's been called the hound of heaven. He will stay on your trail and hunt you down.

In the Hebrew the word for follow is radaph meaning: "to run after, chase, follow, put to flight, hunt, pursue." The action is all on God's part. Think about it, you can follow someone without their even being aware. You can pursue even as they turn their back to you and head in an opposite direction.

If you've ever tried to run from God you know you cannot hide. Even when you are not faithful He can't be anything but faithful. His love for you never fails. His devotion to you is unending, and His kindness follows you wherever you roam.

David says, *Surely goodness and lovingkindness will follow me...* Absolutely, most definitely, without a shadow of a doubt it will follow. For how long, you ask? *All the days of my life,* David answers. Literally, for as long as you have life, all through this earthy one and throughout eternity.

There will be times when the sheep will not understand the methods of the Shepherd, but this truth remains, even then He is good; He is love.

Phillip Keller testifies: "With my natural tendencies to fear, worry and ask 'why,' it was not always simple to assume that he really did know what He was doing with me. There were times I was tempted to panic, to bolt and to leave His care. Somehow I had the strange, stupid notion I could survive better on my own."

Spoken like a true sheep, Mr. Keller, and I should add, it takes one to know one. Near the end of my high school years my Christian family began to fall apart. My parents eventually divorced and I grew angry with God. Surely He deserved the blame. After all, He could have stopped my family's demise and put an end to my pain. I felt like I had done what I was supposed to, but God hadn't come through for me.

In my disillusionment I turned my back on Him, and began to walk away. What I wasn't prepared for, and what truly broke me in the end, was the way He kept loving me. Any direction I turned His goodness and His love whispered to my heart.

What does Paul have to say about the love of Christ? Read 2 Corinthians 5:14-15 and comment.

_____

_____

_____

Our Shepherd's love is the motivating factor in our becoming obedient sheep. We love him because He first loved us. (1 John 4:19)

How does knowing and truly believing that God loves you help you choose to obey Him?

_____

_____

There's something astounding that happens when sheep are loved and cared for day after day by a good shepherd. This same species of animal that can be so stupid (that wool's not white, it's blonde!) can become, when well managed, an incredible asset to the shepherd and his land.

What a metaphor for our lives, sister sheep. As we submit to the guidance of the Good Shepherd His love begins to transform us from the inside out and we become useful for His glory. Did you get that? You are useful to Yahweh. He wants to maximize your potential and do incredible things through you.

> *As we submit to the guidance of the Good Shepherd His love begins to transform us from the inside out and we become useful for His glory.*

Dream big with me for just a moment. We can dream big because we serve a BIG God! If you could do anything, no holds barred, for the Kingdom of God, what would it be?

_____

_____

_____

_____

Look up Jeremiah 32:17 and write this verse out in your own words.

_____

_____

_____

If God can make the heavens and the earth, if His power is that great, and it is, then He can take you, predisposed to panic as you are, and make much of your life. His goodness and His lovingkindness have that effect on His sheep!

I remember a precious chorus we used to sing growing up:

> *"Something beautiful, something good. All my confusion He understood. All I had to offer Him was brokenness and strife, but He made something beautiful of my life."*

What area in your life do you long to see the Shepherd make beautiful? Talk to Him about your desire for an extreme makeover.

_____

_____

And I will dwell in the house of the Lord forever.

David kicks off the Psalm bragging about his Shepherd and he wraps things up with the confident assertion that he will stay on this Shepherd's ranch forever.

My husband Kurt and I have had the indescribable privilege of teaching on a Marriage Retreat Cruise to the Caribbean for the last two years. As I lay reclining on the sandy shore of St. Maarten overlooking about five different shades of blue ocean, enjoying the warm breeze and sipping fresh fruit slushy, I made the comment, "I could stay here forever."

I *could* stay, but I didn't. I came back to reality. David asserts something much different, I *will* stay. His is not a flippant comment based on immediately pleasing circumstances. When David makes up his mind to dwell in the house of the Lord forever he's summing up all that we've talked about in Psalm 23 – the green pastures and quiet waters, yes, but also the unavoidable valleys and enemy attacks as well.

What motivates David to assert his freedom to choose, give up roaming, and stay put? His relationship with the Shepherd, of course. With care this good, why would he ever wander?

> *In daily surrender, even moment by moment surrender, to the Shepherd we trade our panic for peace.*

You know truthfully, this is the crux of the Psalm. Stay or go. Follow the Good Shepherd or a substitute. It's always our choice. I've often said that God is in control, but He's not controlling. Sometimes I wish He would be. "Just force me to stay, Lord. Don't let me venture off."

What does Isaiah 53:6 say about our sheep-like tendency to wander?

Ultimately Christ laid down His life to offer us a spot in His fold. He's done everything to snatch us from our erring ways and bring us to a place of peace. Our first and primary choice is that of accepting Him as our Shepherd, but where daily peace is concerned we have a second surrender to make. Will we stay or will we roam?

These two decisions have faced mankind from the beginning of time. Now you stand at the crossroads. If you have never acknowledged the sacrifice of the Son of God and received Him as your Savior, are you ready to do so today? Simply ask Him to forgive your stubborn, wandering ways and trust Him with your whole heart. This is where peace begins.

Once you can say with David, "The Lord is my Shepherd," then you must purpose to dwell in His presence. Draw near to Him and He will draw near to you. (James 4:8 NASB) *In daily surrender, even moment by moment surrender, to the Shepherd we trade our panic for peace.*

Take time now to respond to one or both of these choices.

_____

_____

And I will dwell in the house of the Lord forever.

The Evangelical Commentary on the Bible states, "The Psalm's last words (Hebrew for length of days) do not suggest (or deny) immortality, but that the welcome and feasting will not be withdrawn while life lasts."

As long as you are alive God welcomes you to call Him Shepherd, to feast with Him, to experience His peace. There is nothing you have ever done or ever will do that can make peace impossible. The Good Shepherd has secured this treasure for you.

For me peace has come to mean staying as close to my Shepherd as possible every single day. After all, forever is comprised of one day at a time. Pardon my paraphrase, but maybe you'll also enjoy saying Psalm 23:6 this way,

> *"...I will dwell in the house of the Lord forever, and I'll do it one day at a time!"*

Reading my Bible, participating in group Bible Studies, keeping a journal for writing down what I hear God saying to me through prayer and His Word, taking advantage of God honoring literature, popping in a worship CD, regular attendance at my church—these are a few of the things that help me nurture the peace I've found.

What actions and activities will help you as you continue choosing to trade panic for peace?

_____

_____

_____

And I will dwell in the <u>house of the Lord</u> forever.

Glance again at Psalm 23:6. Whose house is mentioned?

_____

_____

It's the Lord's house. If I choose to dwell in His house I have to be ok with the fact that He is the Lord. I am not. He is the Shepherd. I am the sheep.

So many of my personal seasons of anxiety have resulted from my desire to be the Shepherd. Let me be blunt, I like being in control. I ride the amusement park's Tilt-a-Whirl with the best of them, but when life starts to tilt and whirl I'm not up for the sensation.

Dwelling in the house of the Lord involves following even when I don't like the house rules. I don't always agree with what God is doing or the way He's going about it! When God and I have a disagreement I've just learned to submit. The amazing thing is He's never once been wrong.

One husband who had been married fifty years jokingly boasted, "I've had the last word in every argument with my wife—'Yes, Ma'am'."

A great deal of peace will be experienced by the sheep who says, "Yes, Sir" to the Shepherd.

Are there any "house rules" you're currently rebelling against? Are there any areas of your heart, your life, that need to respond with a "Yes, Sir" to your Shepherd?

_____

_____

Well who would have believed that six familiar verses could hold so much?

I hope you'll never think of Psalm 23 as just "the funeral Psalm" again!

Bruce Barton said, "There is too much speaking in the world, and almost all of it is too long. The Lord's Prayer, the Twenty-third Psalm, Lincoln's Gettysburg Address, are three great literary treasures that will last forever; no one of them is as long as 300 words. With such striking illustrations of the power of brevity it is amazing that speakers never learn to be brief."

How true! God has said so much to my heart in these few, short verses. I'm confident He's done the same for you. Join me in one last prayer as we borrow the words of hymn writer Dorothy A. Thrupp to express our gratitude.

❀ ❀ ❀

Savior, like a shepherd, lead us. Much we need Thy tender care. In Thy pleasant pastures feed us. For our use Thy folds prepare. Blessed Jesus, blessed Jesus, Thou hast bought us. Thine we art. Blessed Jesus, blessed Jesus, Thou hast bought us. Thine we art.

And now dear sister, may "the Lord bless you, and keep you; the Lord make His face shine upon you, and be gracious to you; the Lord lift up His countenance on you, and give you peace." (Numbers 6:24-26 NASB)

Spiritual Discipline to Practice: Humility

Scripture Passage: Philippians 2:3-4; 1 Peter 5:5-6

Humble pie is hard to swallow. It's definitely an acquired taste and yet God promises sweet rewards for those willing to set aside self and follow the Shepherd.

- ❀ Seek accountability with a godly girlfriend who you trust to be honest with you.

- ❀ Don't think less of yourself. Think of yourself less!

- ❀ Practice complimenting others. Find someone to praise today.

- ❀ Fast from personal pronouns today! Try to get through the day without saying, "I, me or my."

Verse to Memorize: 1 Peter 5:6
"Humble yourselves, therefore, under God's mighty hand, that He may lift you up in due time."

Notes

Notes

Notes

Notes

Chapter 1:

Page 1- STRONG'S EXHAUSTIVE CONCORDANCE OF THE BIBLE, © Copyright 1890 by James Strong, Abingdon Press, Madison, N.J.

Page 5- Spurgeon Quote, The Treasury of David Psalm 23 by Charles H. Spurgeon (Explanatory Notes and Quaint Sayings) as found on the Spurgeon Archive © Copyright 2001 by Phillip Johnson, www.spurgeon.org

Page 6- "Just As I Am" written by Charlotte Elliot, 1835

Page 9- A SHEPHERD LOOKS AT PSALM 23, © Copyright 1970 by W. Phillip Keller, Zondervan Publishing House, Grand Rapids, Michigan

Chapter 2:

Page 16- "I'm In A Hurry (And Don't Know Why)" from Alabama's American Pride Album, RCA, original release 1992; songwriters Roger Murrah and Randy VanWarmer

Page 18- A SHEPHERD LOOKS AT PSALM 23, © Copyright 1970 by W. Phillip Keller, Zondervan Publishing House, Grand Rapids, Michigan

Chapter 3:

Page 29- Baker Quote, The Treasury of David Psalm 23 by Charles H. Spurgeon (Explanatory Notes and Quaint Sayings) as found on the Spurgeon Archive © Copyright 2001 by Phillip Johnson, www.spurgeon.org

Page 29- Spurgeon Quote, The Treasury of David Psalm 23 by Charles H. Spurgeon (Explanatory Notes and Quaint Sayings) as found on the Spurgeon Archive © Copyright 2001 by Phillip Johnson, www.spurgeon.org

Page 35- FORREST GUMP © Copyright 1986 by Winston Groom, Doubleday, Garden City, N.Y.

Page 35- A SHEPHERD LOOKS AT PSALM 23, © Copyright 1970 by W. Phillip Keller, Zondervan Publishing House, Grand Rapids, Michigan

Page 37- EVANGELICAL COMMENTARY ON THE BIBLE, © Copyright 1989 by Walter A. Elwell, Baker Book House, Grand Rapids, Michigan

Chapter 4:

Page 43- Hooper Quote, The Treasury of David Psalm 23 by Charles H. Spurgeon (Explanatory Notes and Quaint Sayings) as found on the Spurgeon Archive © Copyright 2001 by Phillip Johnson, www.spurgeon.org

Page 46- A SHEPHERD LOOKS AT PSALM 23, © Copyright 1970 by W. Phillip Keller, Zondervan Publishing House, Grand Rapids, Michigan

Page 47- UPRISING, © Copyright 2003 by Erwin Raphael McManus, Thomas Nelson, Inc., Nashville, TN

Chapter 5:

Page 60- story as told by Dr. David Jeremiah, CD series Medicine for the Soul available from Turning Point, www.turningpointonline.org

Page 68- EVANGELICAL COMMENTARY ON THE BIBLE, © Copyright 1989 by Walter A. Elwell, Baker Book House, Grand Rapids, Michigan

Pages 69, 75- A SHEPHERD LOOKS AT PSALM 23, © Copyright 1970 by W. Phillip Keller, Zondervan Publishing House, Grand Rapids, Michigan

Page 71- Barth Quote, The Treasury of David Psalm 23 by Charles H. Spurgeon (Explanatory Notes and Quaint Sayings) as found on the Spurgeon Archive © Copyright 2001 by Phillip Johnson, www.spurgeon.org

Page 71- Hardy Quote, The Treasury of David Psalm 23 by Charles H. Spurgeon (Explanatory Notes and Quaint Sayings) as found on the Spurgeon Archive © Copyright 2001 by Phillip Johnson, www.spurgeon.org

Page 77- Burder Quote, The Treasury of David Psalm 23 by Charles H. Spurgeon (Explanatory Notes and Quaint Sayings) as found on the Spurgeon Archive © Copyright 2001 by Phillip Johnson, www.spurgeon.org

Page 77- Quote from 1800's taken from "A plain Explanation of Difficult Passages in the Psalms," 1831, The Treasury of David Psalm 23 by Charles H. Spurgeon (Explanatory Notes and Quaint Sayings) as found on the Spurgeon Archive © Copyright 2001 by Phillip Johnson, www.spurgeon.org

Page 81- "Fill My Cup, Lord" written by Richard Blanchard, 1953

Chapter 6:

Page 86- A SHEPHERD LOOKS AT PSALM 23, © Copyright 1970 by W. Phillip Keller, Zondervan Publishing House, Grand Rapids, Michigan

Page 88- "Something Beautiful" words by Gloria Gaither, music by William J. Gaither, © Copyright 1971

Page 91- EVANGELICAL COMMENTARY ON THE BIBLE, © Copyright 1989 by Walter A. Elwell, Baker Book House, Grand Rapids, Michigan

Page 93- Bruce Barton, 1886-1967

Page 93- "Savior, Like a Shepherd Lead Us" written by Dorothy A. Rupp, 1836

The Lord is my shepherd,
I shall not be in want.

❀ ❀ ❀

Even though I walk
through the valley of the
shadow of death, I will fear
no evil, for you are with
me, your rod and your
staff, they comfort me.

❀ ❀ ❀

He makes me lie down in
green pastures, he leads
me beside quiet waters,...

❀ ❀ ❀

You prepare a table
before me in the
presence of my enemies.
You anoint my head with
oil, my cup overflows.

❀ ❀ ❀

...he restores my soul.
He guides me in paths
of righteousness for
his name's sake.

❀ ❀ ❀

Surely goodness and
love will follow me all
the days of my life, and
I will dwell in the house
of the Lord forever.

❀ ❀ ❀

❀ ❀ ❀

Psalm 23:4
(NIV)

❀ ❀ ❀

- - - - - - - - - - - - - - - - - - - -

❀ ❀ ❀

Psalm 23:1
(NIV)

❀ ❀ ❀
❀

Psalm 23:5
(NIV)

❀ ❀ ❀

- - - - - - - - - - - - - - - - - - - -

❀ ❀ ❀

Psalm 23:2
(NIV)

❀ ❀ ❀

Psalm 23:6
(NIV)

❀ ❀ ❀

- - - - - - - - - - - - - - - - - - - -

❀ ❀ ❀

Psalm 23:3
(NIV)

❀ ❀ ❀

Printed in the United States
201291BV00002B/238-303/A